THE ZOMBIES' ESCAPE

MARCO PELIOTI, A FAMOUS ARCHEOLOGIST, WAS GOING THROUGH THE OLD BOOKS OF HIS GRANDFATHER, WHO WAS ALSO AN ARCHEOLOGIST. SUDDENLY, HE FOUND A SCROLL, ON WHICH WAS THE STORY OF AN ABANDONED VILLAGE NEAR THE POMP VOLCANO, WHERE NUMEROUS VILLAGERS MYSTERIOUSLY DISAPPEARED. IN THE DOCUMENT THERE WAS ALSO A MAP AND THE IMAGE OF A SCEPTER.

MARCO IS ALWAYS IN SEARCH OF NEW ADVENTURES AND MYSTERIOUS STORIES, AND THIS TIME WAS NO DIFFERENT. TOGETHER WITH HIS ADVENTURE PARTNER, TAKKO, HE DECIDED TO INVESTIGATE THE ENIGMA OF THAT VILLAGE AND THE INTRIGUING SCEPTER.

THE NEXT DAY, MARCO AND TAKKO ARRIVED IN THE VILLAGE AND SPOTTED SOME FRIGHTENING STATUES. ACCORDING TO THE INFORMATION ON THE SCROLL, THEY WERE THERE TO WARD OFF CURIOUS PEOPLE.

USING THE MAP ON THE SCROLL, MARCO
FOUND AN ENTRANCE THAT WAS HIDDEN,
UNDER THE PLANTS AND FOLIAGE. WITH THE HELP
OF A FLASHLIGHT, THE PAIR ENTERED THAT DARK
AND GLOOMY ENVIRONMENT.

WHILE SEARCHING FOR CLUES, THE TWO CAME ACROSS MYSTERIOUS DRAWINGS ON THE WALL. THOSE WERE VERY THREATENING FIGURES, WHICH MADE MARCO VERY INTERESTED TO KNOW WHAT THAT MEANT.

JUST AHEAD, TAKKO NOTICED SOMETHING SHINING. AS HE APPROACHED CAREFULLY, HE REALIZED THAT IT WAS A SCEPTER WITH A LUMINOUS STONE. THEN, HE CALLED HIS FRIEND AND SAID: "I FOUND THE SCEPTER FROM THE SCROLL, MARCO!" HE SAID.

THEY WERE HAPPY TO HAVE FOUND THE SCEPTER, THEY REMOVED IT FROM ITS BASE, WHERE THEY NOTICED AN INSCRIPTION. "THIS SCEPTER MUST BE USED TO HELP HUMANITY. WHOEVER TAKES IT FROM ITS REST AND USES IT FOR PERSONAL PURPOSES WILL BE TURNED INTO A ZOMBIE. IF THE JEWEL CEASES TO EXIST IN THE HANDS OF SOMEONE WITH A GOOD HEART, THE ENCHANTMENT WILL END AND THE ZOMBIES WILL VANISH".

SUDDENLY THEY LOOKED AHEAD AND NOTICED A HUGE DOOR. WITH NO HESITATION, MARCO APPROACHED IT, BECAUSE HE WANTED TO OPEN IT.

UPON GETTING CLOSER, MARCO NOTICED THAT THE SCEPTER FITTED PERFECTLY INTO A CRACK IN THE DOOR. THEN HE SLIPPED THE OBJECT INTO PLACE AND EVERYTHING BEGAN TO SHAKE.

THE DOOR OPENED SLOWLY, AND A DENSE SMOKE BEGAN TO EMERGE ALONG WITH A VERY INTENSE LIGHT.

WHEN THE DOOR FINALLY OPENED, SEVERAL FRIGHTENING AND HUNGRY CREATURES APPEARED... THOSE WERE ZOMBIES!

MARCO AND TAKKO RAN OFF!
"WE HAVE TO GET OUT OF HERE AS FAST AS POSSIBLE!
LET'S LOOK FOR AN EXIT!", YELLED MARCO.

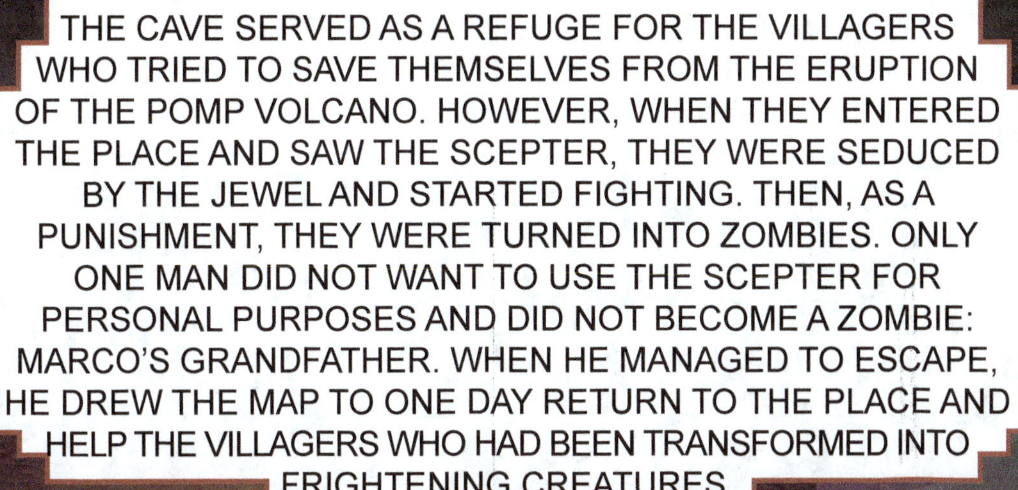

THE CAVE SERVED AS A REFUGE FOR THE VILLAGERS WHO TRIED TO SAVE THEMSELVES FROM THE ERUPTION OF THE POMP VOLCANO. HOWEVER, WHEN THEY ENTERED THE PLACE AND SAW THE SCEPTER, THEY WERE SEDUCED BY THE JEWEL AND STARTED FIGHTING. THEN, AS A PUNISHMENT, THEY WERE TURNED INTO ZOMBIES. ONLY ONE MAN DID NOT WANT TO USE THE SCEPTER FOR PERSONAL PURPOSES AND DID NOT BECOME A ZOMBIE: MARCO'S GRANDFATHER. WHEN HE MANAGED TO ESCAPE, HE DREW THE MAP TO ONE DAY RETURN TO THE PLACE AND HELP THE VILLAGERS WHO HAD BEEN TRANSFORMED INTO FRIGHTENING CREATURES.

SINCE THERE WERE MANY ZOMBIES, MARCO AND TAKKO TRIED TO MISLEAD THEM BY HIDING BEHIND A HUGE COLUMN.

MARCO DECIDED TO LOOK AT THE MAP ON THE SCROLL TO FIND HIS WAY OUT OF THE CAVE. HOWEVER, WHEN MOVING, HE ACCIDENTALLY STEPPED ON A STICK, CRACKING A NOISE. AT THE SAME TIME, THE ZOMBIES HEARD THE NOISE AND FOUND THE TWO FRIENDS
PAK

"RUN! THEY'VE SEEN US AND THEY'RE AFTER US!",
TAKKO SCREAMED. THE TWO SET OFF TOWARD THE
PLACE THEY BELIEVED TO BE
THE EXIT INDICATED ON THE MAP.

ALTHOUGH THE CAVE HAD NUMEROUS PATHS, THE MAP WAS DETAILED AND LED THE TWO CORRECTLY TO THE EXIT.

SENSING THE PRESENCE OF MARCO AND TAKKO, THE ZOMBIES CHASED THEM AT EVERY STEP.

WHEN THEY REACHED THE EXIT, THERE WAS
A LOCKED GATE. BUT, TO THE MISFORTUNE OF
THE TWO FRIENDS, WHEN THEY PULLED THE LEVER,
IT BROKE. "WHATARE WE GOING TO DO NOW?",
TAKKO QUESTIONED

WHEN THE ZOMBIES WERE APPROACHING THEM, MARCO REMEMBERED THE INSCRIPTION ON THE BASE OF THE SCEPTER. "LET'S SEE IF WHAT IS WRITTEN ON THE SCEPTER'S BASE IS RIGHT! THERE WAS WRITTEN THAT, IF THE JEWEL CEASES TO EXIST BY THE HANDS OF SOMEONE WITH A GOOD HEART, THE ENCHANTMENT WILL END AND THE ZOMBIES WILL DISAPPEAR. I JUST HOPE I HAVE A HEART THAT IS GOOD ENOUGH...", HE SAID, HOLDING THE OBJECT

AT THE SAME TIME, MARCO THREW THE SCEPTER AGAINST THE GROUND, SMASHING IT TO PIECES. AND BEING A GOOD-HEARTED PERSON, THE ENCHANTMENT WORKED AND IMMEDIATELY THE JEWEL BEGAN TO EMIT A STRONG BRIGHTNESS.
VUP
POW

THE RAYS EMANATING FROM THE STONE TRAVELED ACROSS THE CAVE FLOOR TOWARDS THE ZOMBIES, HITTING THEM.

THE LIGHTNING BROKE THE ENCHANTMENT AND TURNED THE ZOMBIES INTO NORMAL PEOPLE. THAT PUNISHMENT SERVED AS A LESSON FOR EVERYONE TO UNDERSTAND THAT ONE SHOULD NOT FIGHT OVER ANYTHING OF SUPERFLUOUS VALUE. THEY HAVE LEARNED THAT THEY MUST VALUE LIFE, BECAUSE, AFTER ALL, LOVE AND HAPPINESS ARE THE GREATEST RICHES THERE ARE.

MARCO AND TAKKO THEN BECAME
GREAT HEROES FOR THE PEOPLE OF THE VILLAGE.
WHEN THEY COULD FINALLY RETURN HOME, THE PEOPLE
THREW A BIG PARTY, SINGING AND DANCING WITH THE
PAIR OF FRIENDS.
Vup
Vup
FIM